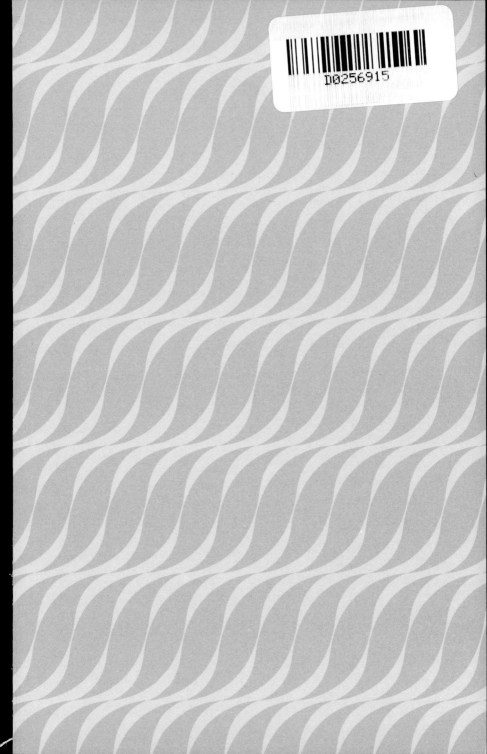

VEGETARIAN GOURMET

Consultant Editor:
Valerie Ferguson

southwater

Contents

Introduction

Not so long ago, gourmet eating was associated only with meat-based meals, but now it is possible to achieve real culinary heights without using meat.

This welcome change has been brought about by our increasing awareness of the best of cuisines from around the world, and also by the ready availability of a wide range of unusual fresh vegetables, salads, herbs, spices, fruit, cereals and pulses, both home-grown and foreign. It is now possible, for example, to buy a variety of cultivated and wild mushrooms, fresh and dried, and with them to create dishes of exceptional subtlety of flavour.

Using this wealth of fine ingredients, *Vegetarian Gourmet* offers recipes for inspirational soups and starters, side dishes and salads, and stunning dishes for entertaining. It is true that some gourmet food takes a little extra time to prepare – you would expect this when cooking for a dinner party or special occasion – but, as the chapter entitled "Easy Gourmet Dishes" shows, it is not always necessary to spend hours in the kitchen to produce vegetarian meals that are truly out of the ordinary. Let this book transport you to new levels of delight in cooking and eating.

Ingredients

Here is a selection of the more unusual vegetables and salad ingredients used in the recipes in this book.

Celeriac

This roughly spherical, knobbly root vegetable has a flavour reminiscent of celery, to which it is related, but with a delicious, nutty undertone. It needs to be peeled before use; the flesh is cream-coloured and crunchy when raw and is a tasty addition to salads. Celeriac scores best as a cooked vegetable, baked in gratins, simmered in soups, steamed or boiled and puréed.

Chicory

A tightly wrapped, pointed bud of elongated leaves, this is most commonly available in its white form (there is also a red chicory), whose colour is achieved by forcing in complete darkness, a technique known as blanching. Its slightly bitter flavour and crisp texture make it an excellent salad vegetable, though it can also be lightly steamed or braised.

Frisée

Also known as Batavian or curly endive, this salad vegetable resembles a ragged-looking lettuce with spiky leaves that are dark green on the outside and paler green in the centre. It tastes quite bitter and is best teamed with milder, sweeter salad ingredients.

Globe Artichoke

Looking rather like a large, green thistle flower tinged with purple, the globe artichoke has an exquisite flavour. There are three parts: the leaves, of which the bottom fleshy section only is eaten, usually dipped in melted butter, Hollandaise sauce or vinaigrette dressing; the inedible hairy choke, which must be discarded; and the tender heart, which is the ultimate treat. If you can find the baby purple artichokes imported from Italy, these only need the tough outer leaves removed and then the whole vegetable can be eaten raw in salads, roasted or cooked in a risotto.

Jerusalem Artichoke

This small, knobbly root vegetable is unrelated to the globe artichoke, despite its similar common name. It has a distinctive, sweet, nutty flavour and makes a particularly fine soup, though it is also good roasted, sautéed, baked in gratins or puréed. Because of its awkward shape, peeling can be time-consuming, though less knobbly varieties are now available.

Mushrooms

Specialist food shops and certain supermarkets are offering a wider variety of mushrooms these days. As well as the usual cultivated button, cap and flat types, you will find brown-cap (or chestnut) mushrooms, wild field mushrooms, yellow, funnel-shaped chanterelles, pale grey-brown oyster mushrooms and ceps (also known by their Italian name, porcini), to name but a few. Oriental shiitake mushrooms, which have a robust flavour, are also widely available.

Button Mushrooms

Ceps

Chanterelles

Pumpkin

Familiar hollowed out as a Hallowe'en lantern, this is a bright orange, spherical vegetable with a tough skin and soft flesh. Pumpkins can grow very large, but it is best to stick to the smaller ones, which have sweeter, less fibrous flesh. They are suitable for both sweet and savoury dishes, such as pies, casseroles and soups. The roasted seeds are edible and nutritious.

Radicchio

This member of the chicory family has densely packed, dark red leaves with thick, white stalks and veins and looks most attractive in salads, though it can also be roasted or sautéed. It has a rather bitter, peppery flavour and a crunchy texture, so should be used sparingly in salads.

Radicchio di Verona

Radicchio di Treviso

Techniques

Skinning & Chopping Tomatoes

It is sometimes recommended that you peel tomatoes before using them.

1 Using a small sharp knife, cut a cross just through the skin at the base of each tomato.

2 Put the tomatoes in a bowl and pour over boiling water. Leave for 20–30 seconds until the skin splits. Drain and transfer to a bowl of cold water. Peel off the skin and chop the flesh into even-size pieces.

COOK'S TIP: Always use firm, fully ripe tomatoes as these will taste better and peel more easily.

Cutting Vegetable Matchsticks

These decorative shapes, also called "julienne", are simple to cut yet look very special.

1 Peel the vegetable and shave off curved edges. Cut across into pieces about 5 cm/2 in long.

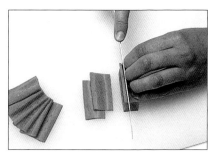

2 Lay each piece flat and cut it lengthways into slices 3 mm/⅛ in thick or less, guiding the side of the knife with your knuckles.

3 Stack the vegetable slices and cut them lengthways into strips about 3 mm/⅛ in thick or less.

Roasting & Peeling Peppers

As peppers have awkward curves, methods of peeling, such as grilling, are easiest. This also heightens the sweetness of the flesh.

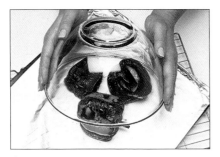

1 Set the peppers on a rack in a grill pan and grill close to the heat. Turn the peppers to char and blister the skin all over. Alternatively, spear each pepper on a long-handled fork and hold it over a flame, turning it slowly so that the skin is charred and blistered on all sides. Put the peppers in a plastic bag and tie it, or place them under a bowl.

2 Cool – the steam trapped inside the bag or bowl will help loosen the skin. When the peppers are cool enough to handle, peel with the help of a small knife.

Blanching & Refreshing

Vegetables are blanched to loosen skins before peeling, to set colour and flavour, and to reduce bitterness. They are often blanched when further cooking is to be done or if they are to be used in a salad. After blanching, most foods are "refreshed" to stop them cooking any further.

1 To blanch: Immerse the food in a large pan of boiling water. Bring the water back to the boil and boil for the time specified, usually 1–2 minutes. Immediately lift the food out of the water, or strain.

2 To refresh: Quickly immerse the food in iced water, or hold under cold running water. If the recipe specifies, leave until it has cooled completely. Drain well.

Gazpacho with Avocado Salsa

A classic chilled soup with a special touch: a topping of chunky, fresh avocado salsa and a scattering of crisp croûtons.

Serves 4

INGREDIENTS
1 cucumber
2 slices day-old bread, soaked in cold water
    for 5 minutes
1 kg/2¼ lb tomatoes, peeled, seeded
    and chopped
1 red pepper, seeded and chopped
1 green chilli, seeded and chopped
2 garlic cloves, chopped
30 ml/2 tbsp extra virgin olive oil
juice of 1 lime and 1 lemon
a few drops Tabasco sauce
600 ml/1 pint/2½ cups
    chilled water
salt and freshly ground
    black pepper
handful of basil leaves,
    to garnish
8 ice cubes, to serve

FOR THE CROÛTONS
2 slices day-old bread,
    crusts removed
1 garlic clove, halved
15 ml/1 tbsp olive oil

FOR THE AVOCADO SALSA
1 ripe avocado
5 ml/1 tsp lemon juice
2.5 cm/1 in piece cucumber, diced
½ red chilli, finely chopped

1 Thinly peel the cucumber, then cut it in half lengthways and scoop out the seeds with a teaspoon. Discard the seeds and chop the flesh.

2 Place the bread, tomatoes, cucumber, red pepper, chilli, garlic, olive oil, citrus juices and Tabasco in a food processor or blender with the water, and blend until well combined but still chunky. Season to taste, and chill for 2–3 hours.

3 To make the croûtons, rub the slices of bread with the garlic clove. Cut the bread into cubes and place in a plastic bag with the olive oil. Seal the bag and shake until the bread cubes are coated with the oil. Heat a large, non-stick frying pan, and fry the croûtons over a medium heat until crisp and golden.

4 Just before serving, make the avocado salsa. Halve the avocado, discard the stone, then peel and dice. Toss the avocado in the lemon juice to prevent it browning, then mix with the cucumber and chilli.

5 Ladle the soup into individual bowls, adding ice cubes to each one. Top the soup with a generous spoonful of the avocado salsa, garnished with the basil leaves. The croûtons should be handed round separately.

Jerusalem Artichoke Soup

A luxurious, creamy soup showcasing the distinctive, nutty taste of this root vegetable, served with Gruyère toasts.

Serves 4–6

INGREDIENTS
25 g/1 oz/2 tbsp butter
30 ml/2 tbsp olive oil
1 large onion, chopped
1 garlic clove, chopped
1 celery stick, chopped
675 g/1½ lb Jerusalem artichokes,
    peeled and chopped
1.2 litres/2 pints/5 cups vegetable stock
300 ml/½ pint/1¼ cups semi-skimmed milk
8 slices French bread
115 g/4 oz/1 cup Gruyère cheese, grated
salt and freshly ground black pepper

1 Heat the butter and oil in a large saucepan, and cook the onion, garlic and celery over a medium heat for about 5 minutes or until softened, stirring occasionally.

2 Add the prepared artichokes and cook for a further 5 minutes.

3 Add the stock and seasoning, bring to the boil, then simmer for 20–25 minutes, stirring occasionally, until the artichokes are tender.

4 Process the soup in a food processor or blender until smooth. Return the soup to the pan, stir in the milk and heat through gently for 2 minutes.

5 Lightly grill the bread on one side, then sprinkle the untoasted side with the Gruyère. Grill until the cheese melts and is golden. Ladle the soup into bowls, and top with the Gruyère toasts.

Celeriac & Spinach Soup

This inspired partnership of vegetables, topped with roasted pine nuts, boasts a wonderful depth of flavour and colour.

Serves 6

INGREDIENTS
1 litre/1¾ pints/4 cups water
250 ml/8 fl oz/1 cup dry white wine
1 leek, thickly sliced
500 g/1¼ lb celeriac, peeled and diced
200 g/7 oz fresh spinach leaves
semi-skimmed milk (optional)
25 g/1 oz/¼ cup pine nuts
sea salt, freshly ground black pepper and
    grated nutmeg

1 Mix the water and wine in a jug. Place the leek, celeriac and spinach in a deep saucepan, and pour over the liquid. Bring to the boil, lower the heat and simmer for 10–15 minutes until the vegetables are soft.

2 Purée the celeriac mixture in a blender or food processor. Return to the clean pan and season to taste with salt, pepper and nutmeg. If the soup is too thick, thin it with a little water or milk. Reheat gently.

3 Roast the pine nuts in a dry, non-stick frying pan until golden. Sprinkle them over the soup and serve.

An Artichoke Lover's Feast

Globe artichokes are a rich, earthy vegetable, which makes a wonderful starter stuffed to the brim with a variety of mushrooms.

Serves 4

INGREDIENTS
4 large globe artichokes
slice of lemon
2 shallots or 1 small onion, chopped
25 g/1 oz/2 tbsp butter
225 g/8 oz/3 cups assorted wild and
    cultivated mushrooms, such as ceps,
    bay boletus, chanterelles, saffron milk-
    caps, oyster mushrooms, St George's,
    Caesar's and closed field mushrooms,
    trimmed and chopped
15 ml/1 tbsp chopped
    fresh thyme

FOR THE HOLLANDAISE SAUCE
175 g/6 oz/³⁄₄ cup unsalted butter
2 egg yolks
juice of ½ lemon
salt and freshly ground
    black pepper

1 Bring a large saucepan of salted water to the boil. With a serrated knife, cut one-third from the top of each artichoke. Pull off the outer leaves and discard. Break off the artichoke stems at the base, then trim about 5 mm/¼ in from the base. To prevent the artichokes from darkening, tie a slice of lemon to the base. Place in the boiling water and cook for 25 minutes.

2 Meanwhile, fry the shallots or onion in the butter to soften but not brown. Add the mushrooms and thyme, cover and cook until the juices begin to run. Increase the heat and allow the juices to evaporate. Remove from the heat and keep warm.

3 When the artichokes are cooked (a small knife inserted in the base will indicate whether it is tender), drain and cool under running water. Remove the lemon slices and drain the artichokes upside down. To create a central cavity, pull out the small leaves from the middle of each artichoke, then scrape out the fibrous choke.

4 To make the hollandaise sauce, melt the butter, skimming off any surface scum. Pour into a jug, leaving behind the milky residue. Place the egg yolks in a glass bowl over a pan of 2.5 cm/ 1 in just simmering water. Add 2.5 ml/½ tsp water to the egg yolks and whisk until thick and foamy.

5 Remove the pan from the heat, then add the butter in a thin stream, whisking all the time. Add the lemon juice and a little boiling water to thin the sauce. Season to taste.

6 Combine one-third of the sauce with the mushroom mixture and use to fill each of the artichokes. Serve at room temperature, with the extra sauce in a separate bowl.

Thai Tempeh Cakes with Sweet Dipping Sauce

Made from soya beans, tempeh is similar to tofu, but has a nuttier taste.
Here, it is combined with a fragrant blend of lemon grass, coriander and
ginger, and formed into small patties.

Makes 8 Cakes

INGREDIENTS

1 lemon grass stalk, outer leaves removed
    and inside finely chopped
2 garlic cloves, chopped
2 spring onions, finely chopped
2 shallots, finely chopped
2 chillies, seeded and finely chopped
2.5 cm/1 in piece fresh root ginger,
    peeled and finely chopped
60 ml/4 tbsp chopped fresh coriander,
    plus extra to garnish
250 g/9 oz/2¼ cups tempeh, defrosted
    if frozen, sliced
15 ml/1 tbsp lime juice
5 ml/1 tsp caster sugar
20 g/¾ oz/3 tbsp plain flour
1 large egg, lightly beaten
salt and freshly ground
    black pepper
vegetable oil, for frying

FOR THE DIPPING SAUCE

45 ml/3 tbsp mirin
45 ml/3 tbsp white wine vinegar
2 spring onions, finely sliced
15 ml/1 tbsp sugar
2 chillies, finely chopped
30 ml/2 tbsp chopped
    fresh coriander
large pinch of salt

1 To make the dipping sauce, mix
together the mirin, white wine
vinegar, sliced spring onions, sugar,
chillies, chopped fresh coriander and
salt in a small bowl. Set aside.

2 Place the lemon grass, garlic, spring
onions, shallots, chillies, ginger and
coriander in a food processor or
blender and process to a coarse paste.
Add the tempeh, lime juice and sugar,
then blend until combined. Add the
flour, egg and seasoning. Process again
until the mixture forms a coarse,
sticky paste.

3 Divide the tempeh mixture into
eight equal parts. Form into balls
with your hands. This mixture will
be quite sticky so it may help to flour
your hands at intervals. Press the balls
flat to form small cakes about 2 cm/
¾ in thick.

4 Heat enough oil to cover the base of a large frying pan. Fry the tempeh cakes for 5–6 minutes, turning once, until golden. Drain the cakes on kitchen paper and serve warm with the dipping sauce, garnished with chopped coriander.

Broccoli Timbales

This elegant, but easy-to-prepare dish makes a superb starter.

Serves 4

INGREDIENTS
butter, for greasing
350 g/12 oz broccoli florets, cooked
45 ml/3 tbsp crème fraîche or
    whipping cream
1 egg, plus 1 egg yolk
15 ml/1 tbsp chopped
    spring onion
pinch of grated nutmeg
salt and freshly ground
    black pepper
fresh chives, to garnish
Hollandaise Sauce,
    to serve (optional)

1 Preheat the oven to 190°C/375°F/ Gas 5. Lightly butter four ramekins. Line the bases with lightly buttered greaseproof paper.

2 Process the cooked broccoli in a food processor with the cream, egg and egg yolk until smooth. Add the spring onion and season with salt, pepper and nutmeg. Pulse to mix.

3 Spoon the purée into the ramekins, place in a water bath and bake for 25 minutes until just set. Invert on to warmed plates and peel off the paper. Garnish with chives, and serve with Hollandaise sauce, if liked.

Cheese & Dill Soufflés

Light as air, these never fail to impress dinner guests.

Serves 6

INGREDIENTS
50 g/2 oz/4 tbsp butter
40 g/1½ oz/⅓ cup plain flour
300 ml/½ pint/1¼ cups milk
115 g/4 oz/1 cup mature Cheddar
   cheese, grated
3 eggs, separated
30 ml/2 tbsp chopped fresh dill
30 ml/2 tbsp grated Parmesan cheese
salt and freshly ground black pepper

1 Preheat the oven to 200°C/400°F/
Gas 6. In a large saucepan, gently
melt the butter and add the flour.
Cook for 2 minutes, stirring
continuously, then gradually add the
milk, stirring. Simmer until thickened,
then allow to cool.

2 Stir the cheese, egg yolks, dill and
seasoning into the sauce. Beat the egg
whites with a pinch of salt until stiff.
Stir one quarter into the cheese sauce,
then fold in the remainder.

3 Butter six small ramekins and dust
with the Parmesan. Divide the mixture
among the ramekins. Bake for 15–20
minutes until the soufflés are puffed
and golden brown. Serve immediately.

Aubergine & Spinach Terrines

Attractive and dainty, these take a little time and patience to assemble, but are perfect for entertaining as they can be prepared well in advance.

Serves 4

INGREDIENTS
1 aubergine
30 ml/2 tbsp extra virgin olive oil
2 courgettes, thinly sliced
leaves from 1 small fresh thyme sprig
4 firm tomatoes, peeled and seeded
4 fresh basil leaves, finely sliced
275 g/10 oz baby spinach leaves
1 garlic clove, crushed
15 g/½ oz/1 tbsp butter
pinch of grated nutmeg
salt and freshly ground black pepper
½ roasted red pepper, skinned and chopped,
   plus a little balsamic vinegar, to serve

1 Preheat the oven to 190°C/375°F/ Gas 5. Seal four 6 cm/2½ in-diameter metal muffin rings at one end with clear film.

2 Slice the aubergine into four equal-sized rounds. Heat half the oil in a frying pan, and fry the slices on both sides until brown. Place them on a baking sheet and cook in the oven for 10 minutes. Transfer to a plate lined with kitchen paper.

3 Heat half the remaining oil in the same pan, and fry the courgettes for 2 minutes, then drain on the kitchen paper. Season with salt and pepper and sprinkle with thyme leaves.

4 Place the tomatoes, basil and the rest of the oil in the frying pan and cook for 5–8 minutes. Cook the spinach, garlic and butter in a saucepan, allowing any liquid to evaporate. Remove from the pan, add the nutmeg and season with salt and pepper.

5 Line the base and about 1 cm/½ in of the sides of the muffin rings with the spinach leaves, making sure the leaves overlap, leaving no gaps. Place the courgettes around the edges of each ring, overlapping slightly.

6 Divide the tomato mixture equally among the rings, pressing down well. Place the aubergines on the top, trimming the edges to fit.

7 Seal the top with clear film, and pierce the base to allow any liquid to escape. Chill overnight. Remove carefully from the rings and serve with diced roasted pepper, drizzled with balsamic vinegar.

Summer Herb & Ricotta Flan

Simple to make and infused with aromatic herbs, this delicate flan makes a delightful lunch dish.

Serves 4

INGREDIENTS
olive oil, for greasing and glazing
800 g/1¾ lb/3½ cups ricotta cheese
75 g/3 oz/1 cup finely grated
    Parmesan cheese
3 eggs, separated
60 ml/4 tbsp torn fresh basil leaves,
    plus a few whole leaves to garnish
60 ml/4 tbsp snipped fresh chives, plus
    extra, to garnish
45 ml/3 tbsp fresh oregano leaves, plus
    extra, to garnish
2.5 ml/½ tsp salt
2.5 ml/½ tsp paprika
freshly ground black pepper

FOR THE TAPENADE
400 g/14 oz/3½ cups pitted black olives,
    rinsed and halved, reserving a few whole
    to garnish (optional)
5 garlic cloves, crushed
75 ml/5 tbsp olive oil

> COOK'S TIP: This flan would be
> perfect for a picnic. Transport in the
> tin and remove at the picnic site.

1 Preheat the oven to 180°C/350°F/ Gas 4, and lightly oil a 23 cm/9 in springform cake tin. Mix together the ricotta, Parmesan and egg yolks in a food processor. Add the herbs and seasoning and blend until smooth.

2 Whisk the egg whites in a large grease-free bowl until they form soft peaks, then gently fold into the ricotta mixture. Spoon into the tin and smooth the top.

3 Bake for 1 hour 20 minutes or until the flan is risen and the top golden. Remove from the oven and brush lightly with olive oil, then sprinkle with paprika. Leave to cool before removing from the tin.

4 To make the tapenade, process the olives and garlic in a food processor until finely chopped. Gradually add the olive oil and blend to a coarse paste, then transfer to a serving bowl. Garnish the flan with chopped chives, basil and oregano leaves and olives, if using, and serve with the tapenade.

Strozzapreti with Courgette Flowers

Scroll-like Strozzapreti is a variety of short pasta from Modena.

Serves 4

INGREDIENTS

50 g/2 oz/4 tbsp butter
30 ml/2 tbsp extra virgin olive oil
1 small onion, thinly sliced
200 g/7 oz small courgettes, cut into thin
    julienne strips
1 garlic clove, crushed
10 ml/2 tsp finely chopped
    fresh marjoram
350 g/12 oz/3 cups dried strozzapreti
1 large handful courgette flowers, thoroughly
    washed and dried, if available
salt and freshly ground
    black pepper
thin shavings of Parmesan
    cheese, to serve

1 Heat the butter and half the oil in a frying pan, and cook the onion gently for 5 minutes. Add the courgettes, garlic, marjoram and seasoning. Cook for 5–8 minutes until the courgettes have softened but are not coloured.

2 Cook the pasta in a pan of salted boiling water until *al dente*. Drain well.

3 Set aside a few courgette flowers for the garnish, then shred the rest and stir into the courgette mixture.

4 Tip the pasta into a warmed bowl and add the remaining oil. Toss and add the courgette mixture. Top with Parmesan and the reserved flowers.

Noodles with Asparagus & Saffron Sauce

A rather elegant, summery dish with fragrant saffron cream.

Serves 4

INGREDIENTS
2 shallots, finely chopped
25 g/1 oz/2 tbsp butter
30 ml/2 tbsp white wine
250 ml/8 fl oz/1 cup
    double cream
pinch of saffron threads, soaked in
    30 ml/2 tbsp boiling water
grated rind and juice of ½ lemon
450 g/1 lb young asparagus
115 g/4 oz peas
350 g/12 oz somen noodles
½ bunch chervil, roughly chopped
salt and freshly ground black pepper
grated Parmesan
    cheese (optional)

1 Cook the shallots in the butter for 3 minutes until soft. Add the wine, cream and saffron infusion. Simmer for 5 minutes or until the sauce thickens to a coating consistency. Add the lemon rind and juice, and season to taste.

2 Cut off the asparagus tips, then slice the remaining spears into short rounds. Blanch the tips, then add them to the sauce. Boil the peas and asparagus rounds until tender and add them to the sauce.

3 Cook the noodles in the same water until just tender. Drain, and toss with the sauce, adding the chervil. Sprinkle with the Parmesan, if using, and serve.

Fresh Herb Risotto

Wild and Italian arborio rice are combined with aromatic herbs to create this creamy, comforting dish.

Serves 4

INGREDIENTS
90 g/3½ oz/½ cup wild rice
1 small onion, finely chopped
15 g/½ oz/1 tbsp butter
15 ml/1 tbsp olive oil
450 g/1 lb/2½ cups arborio rice
300 ml/½ pint/1¼ cups dry
    white wine
1.2 litres/2 pints/5 cups
    vegetable stock
45 ml/3 tbsp chopped fresh oregano
45 ml/3 tbsp snipped fresh chives
60 ml/4 tbsp chopped fresh
    flat-leaf parsley
60 ml/4 tbsp chopped fresh basil
75 g/3 oz/1 cup grated
    Parmesan cheese
salt and freshly ground
    black pepper

1 Cook the wild rice in boiling salted water according to the instructions on the packet.

2 In a large saucepan, cook the onion in the butter and oil for 3 minutes. Add the arborio rice and cook for 2 minutes, stirring.

3 Pour in the wine, bring to the boil and simmer for 10 minutes until the wine is absorbed. Add the stock, a little at a time, and simmer, stirring, for 20–25 minutes until the liquid is absorbed and the rice has a light, creamy texture. Season well.

4 Add the herbs and wild rice. Heat for 2 minutes, stirring. Stir in two-thirds of the Parmesan until melted. Serve, sprinkled with the remaining Parmesan.

COOK'S TIP: Risotto rice is essential to achieve the right creamy texture in this dish. Other types of rice simply will not do. Fresh herbs are also a must, but you can use tarragon, chervil, marjoram or thyme instead of those listed here.

Aubergine & Chick-pea Tagine

Aromatic spices bring a touch of the exotic to this Moroccan–style stew.

Serves 4

INGREDIENTS

1 small aubergine, cut into 1 cm/½ in cubes
2 courgettes, thickly sliced
60 ml/4 tbsp olive oil
1 large onion, sliced
2 garlic cloves, chopped
150 g/5 oz/2 cups brown-cap
    mushrooms, halved
15 ml/1 tbsp ground coriander
10 ml/2 tsp cumin seeds
15 ml/1 tbsp ground cinnamon
10 ml/2 tsp ground turmeric
225 g/8 oz new potatoes, quartered
600 ml/1 pint/2½ cups passata
15 ml/1 tbsp tomato purée
15 ml/1 tbsp chilli sauce
75 g/3 oz/⅓ cup ready-to-eat, unsulphured
    dried apricots
400 g/14 oz/3 cups canned chick-peas,
    drained and rinsed
salt and freshly ground
    black pepper
15 ml/1 tbsp chopped fresh coriander,
    to garnish
steamed couscous, to serve

1 Toss the aubergine and courgettes in 30 ml/2 tbsp of the oil. Grill for 20 minutes, turning occasionally, until tender and golden.

2 Fry the onion and garlic in the remaining oil for 5 minutes until soft, stirring occasionally.

3 Add the halved mushrooms and sauté for 3 minutes until tender. Add the spices and cook for 1 minute more, stirring constantly.

4 Add the potatoes and cook for about 3 minutes, stirring. Pour in the passata, tomato purée and 150 ml/ ¼ pint/⅔ cup water. Cover and cook for 10 minutes or until the sauce begins to thicken.

5 Add the aubergine, courgettes, chilli sauce, apricots and chick-peas. Season and cook, partially covered, for 10–15 minutes until the potatoes are tender. Sprinkle with fresh coriander and serve with couscous.

Radicchio Pizza

This unusual pizza topping consists of chopped radicchio with leeks, tomatoes and Parmesan and Mozzarella cheeses. The base is a scone dough, making this a quick and easy dish to prepare. Serve with a crisp green salad.

Serves 2

INGREDIENTS
200 g/7 oz canned chopped tomatoes
2 garlic cloves, crushed
pinch of dried basil
25 ml/1½ tbsp olive oil, plus extra
    for dipping
2 leeks, sliced
115 g/4 oz radicchio,
    roughly chopped
25 g/1 oz/⅓ cup Parmesan
    cheese, grated
115 g/4 oz Mozzarella cheese, sliced
10–12 black olives, pitted
salt and freshly ground
    black pepper
fresh basil leaves, to garnish

FOR THE DOUGH
225 g/8 oz/2 cups self-raising flour
2.5 ml/½ tsp salt
50 g/2 oz/4 tbsp butter
    or margarine
about 120 ml/4 fl oz/½ cup milk

1 Preheat the oven to 220°C/425°F/ Gas 7, and grease a baking sheet. To make the dough, mix the flour and salt in a bowl, and rub in the butter or margarine. Gradually stir in the milk to form a soft dough.

2 Roll out the dough on a lightly floured surface to make a 25–28 cm/ 10–11 in round. Place on the baking sheet.

3 Pour the tomatoes into a small saucepan. Stir in one of the crushed garlic cloves, together with the dried basil and seasoning. Simmer over a moderate heat until the mixture is thick and reduced by about half.

4 Heat the oil in a large frying pan and fry the leeks and remaining garlic for 4–5 minutes until slightly softened. Add the radicchio and cook, stirring continuously, for a few minutes, then cover and simmer gently for about 5–10 minutes. Stir in the Parmesan, and season with salt and pepper.

5 Cover the dough base with the tomato sauce, and spoon over the leek and radicchio mixture. Arrange the Mozzarella slices on top, and scatter over the black olives. Dip a few basil leaves in olive oil, arrange on the pizza and bake for 15–20 minutes until the scone base and top are golden brown.

Filo "Money Bags" with Creamy Leek Filling

These intriguing and elegant pastries conceal a delicious filling.

Serves 4

INGREDIENTS
115 g/4 oz/½ cup butter
225 g/8 oz/2 cups leeks, trimmed and finely
    chopped
225 g/8 oz/1 cup cream cheese
15 ml/1 tbsp finely chopped fresh dill
15 ml/1 tbsp finely chopped
    fresh parsley
2 spring onions, finely chopped
pinch of cayenne pepper
1 garlic clove, finely chopped
2.5 ml/½ tsp salt
1.5 ml/¼ tsp freshly ground black pepper
1 egg yolk
9 sheets filo pastry, thawed if frozen
lightly cooked leeks, to serve

2 Put the cream cheese in a bowl and stir in the dill, parsley, spring onions, cayenne, garlic and seasoning. Add the egg yolk and leeks and stir well.

3 Melt the remaining butter. Place a sheet of filo pastry on a board, brush with melted butter and place another sheet on top. Brush again with butter and top with a third sheet of filo.

1 Preheat the oven to 200°C/400°F/ Gas 6. Melt 25 g/1 oz/2 tbsp of the butter in a frying pan, and fry the leeks for 4–5 minutes until soft. Drain off any liquid.

4 Cut the layered filo into four squares and place 20 ml/1 rounded tbsp of the cheese mixture in the centre of each square. Gather up the edges into a "bag", twisting the top to seal.

5 Repeat with the other six sheets of filo to make 12 bags in total. Brush each bag with a little more butter.

COOK'S TIP: For an attractive effect, tie each bag with a strip of blanched leek before serving.

6 Place the bags on a greased baking sheet and bake in the oven for 20–25 minutes until golden brown. Serve on a bed of lightly cooked leeks.

Baked Herb Crêpes

These mouth-watering, light herb crêpes make a striking main course.

Serves 4

INGREDIENTS
25 g/1 oz/½ cup chopped fresh herbs (e.g. parsley, thyme and chervil)
15 ml/1 tbsp sunflower oil, plus extra for frying
120 ml/4 fl oz/½ cup skimmed milk
3 eggs
25 g/1 oz/¼ cup plain flour
pinch of salt

FOR THE SAUCE
30 ml/2 tbsp olive oil
1 small onion, chopped
2 garlic cloves, crushed
15 ml/1 tbsp grated fresh ginger root
400 g/14 oz canned chopped tomatoes

FOR THE FILLING
450 g/1 lb fresh spinach
175 g/6 oz/¾ cup ricotta cheese
25 g/1 oz/¼ cup pine nuts, toasted
5 halves sun-dried tomatoes in olive oil, drained and chopped
30 ml/2 tbsp shredded fresh basil
salt, grated nutmeg and freshly ground black pepper
4 egg whites

1 Place the herbs and oil in a blender and blend until smooth. Add the milk, eggs, flour and salt and process again until smooth and pale green. Leave to rest for 30 minutes.

2 Heat a small, non-stick crêpe or frying pan and add a very small amount of oil. Tip out any excess oil and pour in a ladleful of the batter. Swirl around to cover the base of the pan. Cook for 1–2 minutes, turn over and cook the other side. Repeat to make eight crêpes.

3 To make the sauce, heat the oil in a small pan. Add the onion, garlic and ginger and cook gently for 5 minutes until softened. Add the tomatoes and cook for a further 10–15 minutes until the mixture thickens. Purée, sieve and set aside.

4 To make the filling, wash the spinach, discarding any tough stalks, and place in a large pan with only the water that clings to the leaves. Cover and cook, stirring once, until the spinach has just wilted. Remove from the heat and refresh in cold water.

5 Place the spinach in a sieve or colander, squeeze out the excess water and chop finely. Mix with the ricotta, pine nuts, sun-dried tomatoes and basil. Season with salt, nutmeg and freshly ground black pepper.

6 Preheat the oven to 190°C/375°F/Gas 5. Whisk the egg whites until stiff but not dry. Fold one-third into the spinach and ricotta to lighten the mixture, then gently fold in the rest.

7 Place one crêpe at a time on a lightly oiled baking sheet. Put a large spoonful of filling on each and fold into quarters. Repeat until all the crêpes and filling are used up. Bake in the oven for 10–15 minutes or until set. Reheat the tomato sauce and serve with the crêpes.

Twice-baked Spinach & Goat's Cheese Roulade

A roulade is simply a rolled-up soufflé. Because it has air trapped inside, it magically rises again on reheating and becomes quite crisp on the outside.

Serves 4

INGREDIENTS
300 ml/½ pint/1¼ cups milk
50 g/2 oz/½ cup plain flour
150 g/5 oz/9 tbsp butter
100 g/3¾ oz goat's cheese, chopped
40 g/1½ oz/½ cup grated Parmesan cheese,
    plus extra for dusting
4 eggs, separated
250 g/9 oz/3½ cups fresh shiitake
    mushrooms, sliced
275 g/10 oz young spinach leaves, washed
45 ml/3 tbsp crème fraîche or
    fromage frais
salt and freshly ground black pepper

1 Preheat the oven to 190°C/375°F/ Gas 5. Line a 30 x 20 cm/12 x 8 in Swiss roll tin with greaseproof paper, making sure that the paper is well above the sides of the tin as the mixture will rise. Lightly grease.

2 Mix together the milk, flour and 50 g/2 oz/4 tbsp of the butter in a large saucepan. Bring to the boil over a low heat, whisking until thick and creamy. Lower the heat and simmer for 2 minutes, then mix in the goat's cheese and half the Parmesan. Cool for 5 minutes, then beat in the egg yolks and plenty of salt and pepper.

3 Whisk the egg whites in a grease-free bowl until soft peaks form. Carefully fold the whites into the chèvre mixture, using a large metal spoon. Spoon the mixture into the prepared tin, spread gently to level, then bake for 15–17 minutes until the top feels just firm.

4 Let the roulade cool for a few minutes, then invert it on to a sheet of greaseproof paper dusted with Parmesan. Carefully tear off the lining paper in strips. Roll up the roulade in the greaseproof paper and leave to cool completely.

5 Make the filling. Melt the remaining butter in a frying pan and set aside 30 ml/2 tbsp. Add the mushrooms to the pan and stir-fry for 3 minutes. Stir in the spinach and drain well, then add the crème fraîche or fromage frais. Season, then cool.

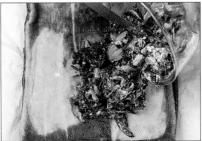

6 Preheat the oven to the original temperature. Unroll the roulade and spread over the filling. Roll it up again and place, join-side down, in a baking dish. Brush with the reserved melted butter and sprinkle with the remaining Parmesan. Bake for 15 minutes or until the roulade is risen and golden. Serve immediately.

Puff Pastry Boxes filled with Spring Vegetables

What could be more tempting than the youngest tender vegetables, bathed in a light Pernod sauce, and served in a crisp pastry case?

Serves 4

INGREDIENTS
225 g/8 oz puff pastry, thawed if frozen
15 ml/1 tbsp grated Parmesan cheese
15 ml/1 tbsp chopped
   fresh parsley
beaten egg, to glaze
175 g/6 oz podded broad beans
115 g/4 oz baby carrots, scraped
4 baby leeks, cleaned
75 g/3 oz/generous ½ cup podded peas,
   thawed if frozen
50 g/2 oz mangetouts, trimmed
salt and freshly ground
   black pepper
fresh dill sprigs, to garnish

FOR THE SAUCE
200 g/7 oz canned chopped tomatoes
25 g/1 oz/2 tbsp butter
25 g/1 oz/¼ cup plain flour
pinch of sugar
45 ml/3 tbsp chopped fresh dill
300 ml/½ pint/1¼ cups water
15 ml/1 tbsp Pernod

1 Preheat the oven to 220°C/425°F/ Gas 7. Lightly grease a baking sheet. Roll out the pastry very thinly. Sprinkle the cheese and parsley over, fold and roll once more, and cut out four 7.5 x 10 cm/3 x 4 in rectangles.

2 Lift the rectangles on to the baking sheet. With a sharp knife, cut an inner rectangle about 1 cm/½ in from the edge of the pastry, cutting halfway through. Score criss-cross lines on top of the inner rectangle, brush with beaten egg and bake for 12–15 minutes until golden.

3 Meanwhile, to make the sauce, press the tomatoes through a sieve into a pan, add the remaining ingredients and bring to the boil, stirring all the time. Lower the heat and simmer until required. Season to taste with salt and pepper.

4 Cook the broad beans in a pan of lightly salted boiling water for about 8 minutes. Add the carrots, leeks and peas, bring back to the boil and cook for a further 5 minutes, then add the mangetouts. Cook for 1 minute. Drain all the vegetables very well.

5 Using a knife, remove the notched squares from the pastry boxes. Set them aside to use as lids. Spoon the vegetables into the pastry cases, pour the sauce over, pop the pastry lids on top and serve immediately, garnished with dill.

Semolina & Pesto Gnocchi

These gnocchi are cooked rounds of semolina paste, which are brushed with melted butter, topped with cheese and baked. They taste wonderful served with a tomato sauce.

Serves 4–6

INGREDIENTS
750 ml/1¼ pints/3⅔ cups milk
200 g/7 oz/generous 1 cup semolina
50 g/2 oz/4 tbsp butter
45 ml/3 tbsp pesto sauce
60 ml/4 tbsp finely chopped sun-dried
    tomatoes, patted dry if oily
75 g/3 oz/1 cup grated
    Pecorino cheese
2 eggs, beaten
grated nutmeg
salt and freshly ground
    black pepper
fresh basil, to garnish
ready-made tomato sauce,
    to serve

1 Heat the milk in a large, non-stick saucepan. When it is on the point of boiling, sprinkle in the semolina, stirring constantly until the mixture is smooth and very thick. Lower the heat and simmer for 2 minutes.

VARIATIONS: Substitute any mature, hard, grating cheese for the Pecorino. Instead of pesto, use a small pack of chopped frozen spinach that has been thawed and squeezed of excess water or 90 ml/ 6 tbsp chopped fresh mixed herbs.

2 Remove from the heat and stir in half the butter, the pesto, sun-dried tomatoes and half the Pecorino. Add the eggs, with nutmeg, salt and pepper to taste. Spoon into a clean, shallow baking dish or tin to a depth of 1 cm/½ in and level the surface. Leave to cool, then chill for 30 minutes.

3 Preheat the oven to 190°C/375°F/ Gas 5. Lightly grease a shallow baking dish. Using a 4 cm/1½ in scone cutter, stamp out as many rounds as possible from the semolina paste.

4 Place the leftover semolina paste on the base of the greased dish, and arrange the rounds on top in overlapping circles. Melt the remaining butter and brush it over the gnocchi. Sprinkle with the remaining Pecorino. Bake for 30–40 minutes until golden. Garnish with basil and serve with the tomato sauce.

Stuffed Baby Vegetables

A dish of heavenly textures and flavours: the flouriness of the potatoes and the smooth richness of the aubergines, united by a spicy masala paste and baked in a tomato sauce laced with fresh coriander.

Serves 4

INGREDIENTS
12 small potatoes
8 baby aubergines
single cream, to garnish (optional)

FOR THE STUFFING
15 ml/1 tbsp sesame seeds
30 ml/2 tbsp ground coriander
30 ml/2 tbsp ground cumin
2.5 ml/½ tsp salt
1.5 ml/¼ tsp chilli powder
2.5 ml/½ tsp ground turmeric
10 ml/2 tsp sugar
1.5 ml/¼ tsp garam masala
15 ml/1 tbsp peanuts, roughly crushed
15 ml/1 tbsp gram flour
2 garlic cloves, crushed
15 ml/1 tbsp lemon juice
30 ml/2 tbsp chopped fresh coriander

FOR THE SAUCE
30 ml/2 tbsp oil
2.5 ml/½ tsp black mustard seeds
400 g/14 oz canned chopped tomatoes
30 ml/2 tbsp chopped
  fresh coriander
150 ml/¼ pint/⅔ cup water

1 Preheat the oven to 200°C/400°F/ Gas 6. Make slits in the potatoes and aubergines, making sure that you do not cut right through.

2 To make the stuffing, mix all the ingredients together on a plate. Carefully stuff the potatoes and aubergines with the spice mixture, and place them in a lightly greased ovenproof dish.

3 To make the sauce, heat the oil in a saucepan and fry the mustard seeds for 2 minutes until they begin to splutter. Add the tomatoes, fresh coriander and any leftover stuffing together with the water. Simmer for 5 minutes until the sauce thickens.

4 Pour the sauce over the potatoes and aubergines. Cover and bake for 25–30 minutes until the potatoes and aubergines are soft. Garnish with single cream, if using, and serve.

Coriander Ravioli with Pumpkin Filling

A stunning, fresh herb pasta with a superb, creamy pumpkin and roast garlic filling – perfect for an autumn dinner party.

Serves 4–6

INGREDIENTS
200 g/7 oz/scant 2 cups strong unbleached white flour
2 eggs
pinch of salt
45 ml/3 tbsp chopped fresh coriander
fresh coriander sprigs, to garnish

FOR THE FILLING
4 garlic cloves, unpeeled
450 g/1 lb pumpkin, peeled and seeded
115 g/4 oz/½ cup ricotta cheese
4 halves sun-dried tomatoes in olive oil, drained and finely chopped, 30 ml/2 tbsp of the oil reserved
freshly ground black pepper

1 Place the flour, eggs, salt and coriander into a food processor. Pulse until combined to form a soft dough.

2 Transfer the dough to a lightly floured surface and knead well for 5 minutes until smooth. Wrap in clear film and leave to rest in the fridge for 20 minutes.

3 To make the filling, preheat the oven to 200°C/400°F/Gas 6. Place the garlic cloves on a baking sheet and bake for 10 minutes until softened.

4 Steam the pumpkin pieces for 5–8 minutes until tender and drain well. Peel the garlic cloves and mash into the pumpkin, together with the ricotta and drained sun-dried tomatoes. Season with black pepper.

5 Divide the dough into four pieces and flatten slightly. Using a pasta machine on its thinnest setting, roll out each of the four pieces. Leave the sheets of pasta on a clean dish towel until slightly dried.

6 Using a 7.5 cm/3 in, crinkle-edged, round cutter, stamp out 36 rounds. Top 18 of the rounds with a teaspoonful of the pumpkin mixture, brush the edges with water, and place another round of pasta on top. Press firmly around the edges to seal.

7 Bring a large pan of water to the boil, add the ravioli and cook for 3–4 minutes. Drain well and toss with the reserved tomato oil. Serve garnished with coriander sprigs.

45

Wild Mushroom Brioche with an Orange Butter Sauce

This butter-rich brioche, stuffed full of flavoursome fungi, is served with a luxurious sauce, and accompanied by a green salad.

Serves 4

INGREDIENTS
5 ml/1 tsp active dried yeast
45 ml/3 tbsp milk, at room temperature
400 g/14 oz/3½ cups strong
    white flour
5 ml/1 tsp salt
15 ml/1 tbsp caster sugar
3 eggs
finely grated rind of ½ lemon
200 g/7 oz/scant 1 cup unsalted butter,
    at room temperature

FOR THE FILLING
2 shallots, chopped
50 g/2 oz/4 tbsp unsalted butter
350 g/12 oz/4½ cups assorted wild and
    cultivated mushrooms, such as ceps,
    bay boletus, chanterelles,
    winter chanterelles, saffron milk-caps,
    oyster mushrooms and horn of plenty,
    trimmed, sliced and roughly chopped
½ garlic clove, crushed
75 ml/5 tbsp chopped fresh parsley
salt and freshly ground
    black pepper

FOR THE ORANGE BUTTER SAUCE
30 ml/2 tbsp frozen orange
    juice concentrate
175 g/6 oz/¾ cup unsalted butter, diced
salt and cayenne pepper

1 Dissolve the yeast in the milk, add 115 g/4 oz/1 cup of the flour and mix to form a dough. Fill a bowl with hand-hot water, then place the dough in the water. Leave for 30 minutes to activate the yeast.

2 Place the remaining flour in a food processor fitted with the dough blade, and add the salt, sugar, eggs, lemon rind and the risen dough and process briefly to mix. Add the butter in small pieces and process until the dough is silky smooth and very slack. Lift the dough out on to a sheet of clear film, wrap and chill for 2 hours until firm.

3 To make the filling, fry the shallots in the butter without letting them brown. Add the mushrooms and garlic, allow the juices to run, and then increase the heat to reduce the moisture. When dry, turn into a bowl, add the parsley and season. Chill.

4 Grease a 900 g/2 lb loaf tin and line with non-stick baking paper. Roll out the dough on a floured surface to form a rectangle 15 x 30 cm/6 x 12 in. Spoon the mushroom filling over the dough and roll up.

5 Drop the dough into the loaf tin, cover with a damp dish towel and leave to rise in a warm, humid place for 50 minutes.

6 Preheat the oven to 190°C/375°F/ Gas 5. When the dough has risen above the rim of the tin, place in the oven and bake for 40 minutes.

7 To make the sauce, place the orange juice concentrate in a heatproof glass bowl and heat by standing in a saucepan of simmering water. Remove the pan from the heat and whisk the butter into the juice until creamy. Season to taste, cover and keep warm. Turn out the cooked brioche, slice and serve with the sauce and a green salad.

Peas with Baby Onions & Cream

Ideally, use fresh peas for this side dish with a touch of luxury.

Serves 4

INGREDIENTS
175 g/6 oz baby onions
15 g/½ oz butter
900 g/2 lb fresh peas (about 350 g/12 oz shelled or frozen)
150 ml/¼ pint/⅔ cup double cream
30 ml/2 tbsp plain flour
10 ml/2 tsp chopped fresh parsley
15–30 ml/1–2 tbsp lemon juice (optional)
salt and freshly ground black pepper

1 Peel the onions and halve them if necessary. Melt the butter in a flameproof casserole, and fry the onions for 5–6 minutes over a moderate heat until they begin to be flecked with brown.

2 Add the peas and stir-fry for a few minutes. Add 120 ml/4 fl oz/½ cup water and bring to the boil. Partially cover the casserole and simmer for about 10 minutes until both the peas and onions are tender. There should be a thin layer of water on the base of the pan.

3 Using a small whisk, blend the cream with the flour. Remove the pan from the heat, and stir in the combined cream and flour. Add the parsley and season to taste.

4 Cook over a gentle heat for about 3–4 minutes until the sauce is thickened. Taste, and adjust the seasoning; add a little lemon juice to sharpen, if liked. Serve hot.

Roasted Potatoes, Peppers & Shallots

Cooked together, these vegetables lend their flavours to each other.

Serves 4

INGREDIENTS
500 g/1¼ lb waxy potatoes
12 shallots
2 yellow peppers
olive oil
2 fresh rosemary sprigs
salt and freshly ground
   black pepper

1 Preheat the oven to 200°C/400°F/ Gas 6. Wash the potatoes and blanch for 5 minutes in boiling water. Drain and, when they are cool enough to handle, skin them and cut them in half lengthways.

2 Soak the shallots in boiling water for 2 minutes. Drain and peel them. Cut each yellow pepper lengthways into eight strips, discarding the seeds and pith.

3 Oil a shallow, ovenproof dish thoroughly. Assemble the potatoes and peppers in the dish in alternating rows and stud with the shallots.

4 Cut the rosemary sprigs into 5 cm/2 in lengths and tuck among the vegetables. Sprinkle the dish with olive oil and seasoning, and bake, uncovered, for 30–40 minutes until all the vegetables are tender. Serve hot.

Lemony Vegetable Parcels

This method of baking root vegetables sealed in paper produces a light result which is nonetheless mouthwatering. Allow diners to open their own "parcel" at the table and enjoy the aroma as it is released.

Serves 4

INGREDIENTS
2 medium carrots
1 small swede
1 large parsnip
1 leek, sliced
finely grated rind of ½ lemon
15 ml/1 tbsp lemon juice
15 ml/1 tbsp wholegrain mustard
5 ml/1 tsp walnut or
    sunflower oil
salt and freshly ground
    black pepper

2 Stir the lemon rind, lemon juice and the mustard into the vegetables and mix well. Season to taste with salt and pepper.

1 Preheat the oven to 190°C/375°F/ Gas 5. Peel the carrot, swede and parsnip, and cut into 1 cm/½ in cubes. Place in a large bowl, then add the sliced leek.

3 Cut four 30 cm/12 in squares of non-stick baking paper and brush lightly with the oil.

VARIATION: Other vegetables in season can be cooked in this way. Try courgettes, sweet peppers and asparagus in the summer.

4 Divide the vegetables among the paper squares. Roll up each square from one side, then twist the ends firmly to seal.

5 Place the sealed parcels on a baking sheet and bake for 50–55 minutes or until the vegetables are just tender when pierced with a knife. Serve hot.

Courgette & Carrot Ribbons

This colourful vegetable combination is served in a herby cheese sauce.

Serves 4

INGREDIENTS
1 large green pepper, seeded
  and diced
15 ml/1 tbsp sunflower oil
225 g/8 oz Brie cheese
30 ml/2 tbsp crème fraîche
5 ml/1 tsp lemon juice
60 ml/4 tbsp milk
10 ml/2 tsp freshly ground
  black pepper
30 ml/2 tbsp very finely chopped
  fresh parsley, plus extra,
  to garnish
salt
6 large courgettes
6 large carrots

1 Sauté the green pepper in the oil until just tender. Place all the remaining ingredients, except the carrots and courgettes, in a food processor and blend well. Place the mixture in a saucepan and add the green pepper.

2 Peel the courgettes and carrots and slice them into long, thin strips. Simmer for 3 minutes in separate saucepans until barely cooked.

3 Heat the green pepper and cheese mixture and pour into a shallow vegetable dish. Toss the courgette and carrot strips together and arrange them in the sauce. Garnish with chopped parsley and serve.

Stuffed Tomatoes with Wild Rice

A dish which also makes a fine light meal with crusty bread and a salad.

Serves 4

INGREDIENTS
8 medium tomatoes
50 g/2 oz/⅓ cup sweetcorn kernels
30 ml/2 tbsp white wine
50 g/2 oz/¼ cup cooked wild rice
1 garlic clove
50 g/2 oz/½ cup grated Cheddar cheese
15 ml/1 tbsp chopped fresh coriander
salt and freshly ground black pepper
15 ml/1 tbsp olive oil

1 Cut the tops off the tomatoes and remove the seeds using a teaspoon. Scoop out all the flesh and chop finely; also chop the tops.

2 Preheat the oven to 180°C/350°F/ Gas 4. Put the chopped tomatoes in a pan and add the sweetcorn and wine. Cover with a close-fitting lid and simmer until tender. Drain.

3 Mix together all the remaining ingredients except the oil, adding salt and pepper to taste. Carefully spoon the mixture into the tomatoes, piling it higher in the centre to prevent it from overflowing.

4 Sprinkle the oil over the top, arrange the tomatoes in an ovenproof dish and bake for 15–20 minutes until cooked through. Serve immediately.

Roast Mediterranean Vegetables with Pecorino

Aubergines, courgettes, peppers and tomatoes make a marvellous medley when roasted and served drizzled with fragrant olive oil. Shavings of Pecorino cheese add the perfect finishing touch.

Serves 4–6

INGREDIENTS
1 aubergine, sliced
2 courgettes, sliced
2 peppers (red or yellow or one of each),
    seeded and quartered
1 large onion, thickly sliced
2 large carrots, cut into sticks
4 firm plum tomatoes, halved
extra-virgin olive oil
45 ml/3 tbsp chopped
    fresh parsley
45ml/3 tbsp pine nuts,
    lightly toasted
115 g/4 oz piece Pecorino cheese
salt and freshly ground
    black pepper
crusty bread, to serve (optional)

1 Layer the aubergine slices in a colander, sprinkling each layer with a little salt. Leave to drain over a sink or plate for about 20 minutes, then rinse thoroughly, drain well and pat dry with kitchen paper. Preheat the oven to 220°C/425°F/Gas 7.

VARIATION: Any hard cheese can be used for the topping. Try Spanish Manchego or British Malvern.

2 Spread out all the vegetables in one or two large roasting tins. Brush lightly with olive oil and roast in the oven for about 20 minutes, or until lightly browned and the skins on the peppers have begun to blister.

3 Transfer the vegetables to a large serving platter. If you like, peel the peppers. Trickle over any vegetable juices from the pan, and drizzle over some more oil. Season with salt and freshly ground black pepper.

4 When the vegetables are at room temperature, mix in the chopped fresh parsley and toasted pine nuts.

5 Using a vegetable peeler, shave the Pecorino and scatter the shavings over the vegetables. Serve with crusty bread, if you wish, as a starter, or as an accompaniment for a buffet or barbecue.

Radish, Mango & Apple Salad

This salad is full of clean, crisp tastes and distinctive flavours.

Serves 4

INGREDIENTS
10–15 radishes
1 dessert apple, peeled, cored and
    thinly sliced
2 celery sticks, thinly sliced
1 small ripe mango
fresh dill sprigs, to garnish

FOR THE DRESSING
120 ml/4 fl oz/½ cup
    soured cream
10 ml/2 tsp creamed horseradish
15 ml/1 tbsp chopped fresh dill
salt and freshly ground
    black pepper

1 To make the dressing, blend together the soured cream, horseradish and dill in a small jug or bowl and season with a little salt and pepper.

2 Top and tail the radishes and slice them thinly. Place in a bowl, together with the apple and celery.

3 Cut through the mango lengthways either side of the stone. Make even criss-cross cuts through each side section, then bend it back to separate the cubes, and add to the bowl.

4 Pour the dressing over the vegetables and fruit and stir gently so that all the ingredients are coated. When ready to serve, garnish with sprigs of dill.

Asparagus & Orange Salad

A good-quality olive oil is essential for this refreshing, summery salad.

Serves 4

INGREDIENTS
225 g/8 oz asparagus, trimmed and cut into
    5 cm/2 in pieces
2 large oranges
2 well-flavoured tomatoes, cut into eighths
50 g/2 oz romaine lettuce
    leaves, shredded
30 ml/2 tbsp extra-virgin olive oil
2.5 ml/½ tsp sherry vinegar
salt and freshly ground black pepper

1 Cook the asparagus in boiling salted water for 3–4 minutes until just tender. Drain and refresh under cold water.

2 Grate the rind from half an orange and reserve. Peel both the oranges and cut into segments between the membrane. Squeeze the juice from the remaining membrane and reserve.

3 Put the asparagus, orange segments, tomatoes and lettuce into a salad bowl. Mix together the oil and vinegar, add 15 ml/1 tbsp of the reserved orange juice and 5 ml/1 tsp of the grated rind. Season with salt and freshly ground black pepper.

4 Just before serving, pour the dressing over the salad and mix gently to coat.

Watercress & Walnut Salad

Blue Roquefort and sweet pears are perfect partners in this salad.

Serves 6

INGREDIENTS
75 g/3 oz/½ cup shelled walnuts, halved
2 red Williams pears, cored and sliced
15 ml/1 tbsp lemon juice
150 g/5 oz/1 large bunch watercress, tough stalks removed
200 g/7 oz/scant 2 cups Roquefort cheese, cut into chunks

FOR THE DRESSING
45 ml/3 tbsp extra virgin olive oil
30 ml/2 tbsp lemon juice
2.5 ml/½ tsp clear honey
5 ml/1 tsp Dijon mustard
salt and freshly ground black pepper

1 Toast the walnuts in a dry frying pan. Toss frequently until golden.

2 Make the dressing. Place the olive oil, lemon juice, honey, mustard and seasoning in a bowl or screw-top jar. Stir or shake vigorously to combine.

3 Toss the pear slices in the lemon juice and add the watercress, walnuts and Roquefort. Toss the dressing with the salad and serve.

Right: Watercress & Walnut Salad (top); Tomato & Bread Salad

Tomato & Bread Salad

Italian-style bread is essential for this colourful, classic Tuscan salad.

Serves 6

INGREDIENTS
275 g/10 oz/10 slices day-old Italian-style bread, thickly sliced
1 cucumber, peeled and cut into chunks
5 tomatoes, seeded and diced
1 large red onion, chopped
200 g/7 oz/generous 1 cup good-quality olives
20 fresh basil leaves, torn

FOR THE DRESSING
60 ml/4 tbsp extra virgin olive oil
15 ml/1 tbsp red or white wine vinegar
salt and freshly ground black pepper

1 Soak the bread in water for about 2 minutes, then lift out and squeeze gently, first with your hands and then in a tea towel to remove any excess water. Chill for 1 hour.

2 Meanwhile, to make the dressing, place the oil, vinegar and seasoning in a bowl or screw-top jar. Stir or shake vigorously to combine.

3 Place the cucumber, tomatoes, onion and olives in a bowl. Break the bread into chunks and add to the bowl with the basil. Toss the dressing with the salad before serving.

Fruit & Raw Vegetable Gado-gado

Line the platter with a banana leaf, which can be bought from Asian stores, instead of the mixed salad leaves if you wish to serve this Indonesian-inspired dish for a special occasion.

Serves 6

INGREDIENTS
½ cucumber, peeled
2 pears (not too ripe)
1–2 dessert apples
juice of ½ lemon
mixed salad leaves
6 small tomatoes, cut into wedges
3 slices fresh pineapple, cored and cut into wedges
3 eggs, hard-boiled, shelled and quartered or sliced
175 g/6 oz egg noodles, cooked, cooled and chopped
deep-fried onions, to garnish

FOR THE PEANUT SAUCE
2–4 fresh red chillies, seeded and very finely chopped
300 ml/½ pint/1¼ cups coconut milk
350 g/12 oz/1½ cups crunchy peanut butter
15 ml/1 tbsp dark soy sauce or dark brown sugar
5 ml/1 tsp tamarind pulp, soaked in 45 ml/3 tbsp warm water or 15 ml/1 tbsp lemon juice
coarsely crushed peanuts
salt

1 To make the peanut sauce, put the chillies in a pan, pour in the coconut milk, then stir in the crunchy peanut butter. Heat gently, stirring, until well blended.

2 Simmer gently until the sauce thickens, then stir in the soy sauce or sugar. Strain in the tamarind juice, add salt to taste and stir well. Spoon into a bowl and sprinkle with a few coarsely crushed peanuts.

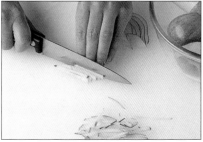

3 Core the cucumber and peel the pears. Cut both into matchsticks. Finely shred the apples and sprinkle them with the lemon juice. Spread a bed of salad leaves on a platter, then pile the fruit and vegetables on top.

4 Add the hard-boiled eggs, noodles and deep-fried onions. Serve at once, with the sauce.

Cracked Wheat & Mint Salad

Cracked wheat has been partially cooked, so it requires only a short soaking before serving.

Serves 4

INGREDIENTS
250 g/9 oz/1½ cups cracked wheat
4 tomatoes, peeled, seeded and
    roughly chopped
4 small courgettes, thinly sliced lengthways
4 spring onions, sliced on
    the diagonal
8 ready-to-eat dried apricots, chopped
40 g/1½ oz/¼ cup raisins
juice of 1 lemon
30 ml/2 tbsp tomato juice
45 ml/3 tbsp chopped fresh mint
1 garlic clove, crushed
salt and freshly ground black pepper
fresh mint sprig, to garnish

1 Put the cracked wheat into a large bowl. Add enough cold water to come 2.5 cm/1 in above the level of the wheat. Leave to soak for 30 minutes, then drain well and squeeze out any excess water in a clean dish towel.

2 Stir the chopped tomatoes, courgettes, spring onions, apricots and raisins into the cracked wheat.

3 Put the lemon and tomato juice, mint, garlic and seasoning into a small bowl and whisk together with a fork. Pour over the salad and mix well. Chill in the fridge for at least 1 hour. Serve garnished with a sprig of mint.

Lentil, Tomato & Cheese Salad

Lentils and cheese are a natural combination. The small, blue-green Puy lentils from France are perfect for salads.

Serves 6

INGREDIENTS

200 g/7 oz/scant 1 cup lentils (preferably Puy), soaked for about 3 hours in cold water to cover
1 red onion, chopped
1 bay leaf
60 ml/4 tbsp extra-virgin olive oil
45 ml/3 tbsp chopped fresh parsley
30 ml/2 tbsp chopped fresh oregano or marjoram
250 g/9 oz cherry tomatoes, halved
250 g/9 oz feta, goat's cheese or Caerphilly, crumbled
chicory or frisée leaves
salt and freshly ground black pepper
fresh herbs, to garnish
30–45 ml/2–3 tbsp lightly toasted pine nuts, to serve

1 Drain the lentils and place them in a large saucepan. Pour in plenty of cold water and add the onion and bay leaf. Bring to the boil, boil hard for 10 minutes, then lower the heat and simmer for 20 minutes or according to the instructions on the packet.

2 Drain the·lentils, discarding the bay leaf, and tip them into a bowl. Add salt and pepper to taste. Toss with the olive oil. Set aside to cool, then stir in the fresh parsley, oregano or marjoram and cherry tomatoes.

3 Add the cheese. Line a serving dish with the chicory or frisée leaves and pile the salad in the centre. Scatter over the pine nuts, garnish with fresh herbs and serve.

This edition published by Southwater

Distributed in the UK by
The Manning Partnership, 251-253 London Road East,
Batheaston, Bath BA1 7RL, UK
tel. (0044) 01225 852 727 fax. (0044) 01225 852 852

Distributed in Australia by
Sandstone Publishing, Unit 1, 360 Norton Street,
Leichhardt, New South Wales 2040, Australia
tel. (0061) 2 9560 7888 fax. (0061) 2 9560 7488

Distributed in New Zealand by
Five Mile Press NZ, PO Box 33-1071,
Takapuna, Auckland 9, New Zealand
tel. (0064) 9 4444 144 fax. (0064) 9 4444 518

Southwater is an imprint of Anness Publishing Limited

© 2000 Anness Publishing Limited

A CIP catalogue record for this book
is available from the British Library.

1 3 5 7 9 10 8 6 4 2

Publisher: Joanna Lorenz
Editor: Valerie Ferguson
Series Designer: Bobbie Colgate Stone
Designer: Andrew Heath
Editorial Reader: Jonathan Marshall
Production Controller: Joanna King

Recipes contributed by: Catherine Atkinson,
Michelle Berriedale-Johnson, Kit Chan,
Jacqueline Clark, Frances Cleary, Carole Clements,
Roz Denny, Patrizia Diemling, Christine France,
Nicola Graimes, Deh-Ta Hsuing, Christine Ingram,
Manisha Kanani, Ruby Le Bois, Norma Miller,
Sallie Morris, Annie Nichols, Katherine Richmond,
Steven Wheeler, Elizabeth Wolf-Cohen,
Jeni Wright.

Photography: Karl Adamson, Mickie Dowie,
James Duncan, John Freeman, Michelle Garrett,
John Heseltine, Amanda Heywood,
Janine Hosegood, David Jordan,
William Lingwood, Patrick McLeavey,
Thomas Odulate.

Notes:
For all recipes, quantities are given in both metric
and imperial measures and, where appropriate,
measures are also given in standard cups
and spoons.
Follow one set, but not a mixture, because they
are not interchangeable.

Standard spoon and cup measures are level.

1 tsp = 5 ml   1 tbsp = 15 ml

1 cup = 250 ml/8 fl oz

Australian standard tablespoons are 20 ml.
Australian readers should use 3 tsp in place of
1 tbsp for measuring small quantities of gelatine,
cornflour, salt, etc.

Medium eggs are used unless otherwise stated.

Printed and bound in Singapore